WOMAN WITH CROWS

WOMAN WITH CROWS

poems by
RUTH THOMPSON

SADDLE ROAD PRESS

Woman with Crows
(Revised Edition)
© 2013 by Ruth Thompson

Saddle Road Press
Hilo, Hawai'i
http://saddleroadpress.com

Cover and author photographs by Don Mitchell

ISBN 978-0-9833072-8-0

Library of Congress Control Number: 2013917688

Also by Ruth Thompson

Here Along Cazenovia Creek (Saddle Road Press 2011)

Woman with Crows was originally published
by Word Press in 2012.

In memory of my grandmother, Bessie
and
for my daughter, Rachel

CONTENTS

I. WOMAN WITH CROWS

WOMAN WITH CROWS	13
LETTING IT GO	14
SECOND CHILDHOOD	16
WISE TO CINDERELLA	17
FAT TIME	18
MYOPIA IN THE AFTERNOON	20
FIREWORKS	21
BLESS YOU, FATHER WALT	22
OLD PLOW HORSES	23
NOVEMBER BY CAZENOVIA CREEK	24
SUDDEN OAK DEATH SYNDROME	25
THE OWL	26
SPEAKING OF THE MUSE	27

II. THE HUNGRY GHOST

BIRTH OF THE HUNGRY GHOST	31
THE WITCH RAPUNZEL	32
DEATH OF THE HUNGRY GHOST	33
GRIMM GHOST	34
GRAVE OF THE HUNGRY GHOST	35
CODA	36
WHY HUNGRY GHOSTS MUST KEEP FLYING	37

III. SLEEPING BEAUTY

SLEEPING BEAUTY	41
THE FINNMAN	42
WHAT SHE LOST	43
IN THE COUNTRY OF THE DEAD	44

THE BUTTERFLY GIRL IS DEAD BETWEEN THE EARS 45
LOCAL HABITATION   46
MY HUMP SPEAKS   47
JILL AND THE BEANSTALK   48
THE ENDING   49
SONG FOR A DEAD MAN   50
INANNA RETURNS   51
WHAT THE RIVER SAYS   52

IV. IN MY GRANDMOTHER'S GARDEN

EASTER MORNING   55
IN MY GRANDMOTHER'S GARDEN   56
MEMORY OF BESSIE FRAMED IN A MIRROR   57
THE INVENTOR OF THE LUVAILEAN SONNET   58
OUR FATHER'S DEAFNESS   60
LISTENING   61
TRANSLATIONS   62

V. PERSEPHONE TELLS ALL

RUMPELSTILTSKIN   65
CRONE STORY   66
PERSEPHONE TELLS ALL   67
THE REAL STORY   69
THE MERMAID SINGS   71

VI. MONKEYPOD SUITE

HILO FARMERS' MARKET   75
MY FAT ZUMBA TEACHER   77
MONKEYPOD SUITE   78
EL NIÑO WINTER, HILO   80
ON HILO BAY   81

TRADEWIND RAIN   82
WALKING AKOLEA ROAD   83

VII. PACKING FOR THE JOURNEY

PACKING FOR THE JOURNEY   87
FOOL ON THE BANK OF THE RIVER STYX   88
THE WHITE QUEEN   89
MY LIFE IN MATHEMATICS   91
A MAY AFTERNOON AT THE POETS' GROUP   93
DRIFTWOOD   95
SOMEONE WILL REMEMBER US   96
ON SANTA MONICA BEACH   97
HUMUS   98

VIII. SOMETIMES IN DREAMS

JOURNEYING WEST   101
TRAVEL INSTRUCTIONS FOR ELMWOOD AVENUE   103
FOR CIRCE   104
AT GHOST RANCH   105
I AM HERE TO TELL YOU   106
DREAM OF THE SNOW LEOPARD   107
MINE   108
SOMETIMES IN DREAMS YOU SEE WINGS   109

I. Woman With Crows

WOMAN WITH CROWS

There is a woman who catches crows on her tongue.
They speak when she is tongue-tied.

In the mornings she advises balloons. How high it is
safe to go, and when to retire from politics.

At night she turns into creek water and sleeps in a
quart berry basket. A crow could carry her.

When she awakens, she unfolds her tail. She sticks
out her tongue. The crows come down in a cloud
of balloons.

Letting It Go

I'm walking on my birthday
and this time
I'm
letting it go.

Headline!
Waistline!
Toe the line!
Morning line!

I've stopped stopping
at all the roads not taken
(you know the ones I mean)

because here's the joke:
every road is a dead end.

So I'm just walking on my birthday
and letting it go.

In my throat, regret.
On my tongue, mourning...

but here's coyote brush with the dew still on it,
and black sage, and sumac —
has anything ever smelled so good?

Here's clay dust under foot, a little hot already,
sunshine clapping me on the shoulder —

and here's a sky the exact blue of a '57 Chevy,
dog grinning over his shoulder,
jaybird yammering like no tomorrow —

and here I am!
And it's my birthday!
And right this minute
I'm walking.

Second Childhood

Bless Lucille's big hips!
And bless my own free-at-last hips!
Here they are dawdling
and not worrying one
bit about where they are
in relation
to anyone else.

You can look at me or not.
I am not saying anything personal anymore.

I am saying hips breasts belly legs feet
roots branches and big thick trunk
tides
sunrises
monkeys lithe and witty in the dawn trees
tigers shaking out oiled stripes of sun and shadow —

I say you can look at me or not.
I am busy dancing —
freckled
and fond
and fat as the fat old sun.

WISE TO CINDERELLA

for Mary Brown

At five, we liked the same stories,
laughed at dissonance, were wise to Cinderella.

We dressed in women's clothes, tried them on
for size. No tulle or glass slippers,
though we'd have gone for a spangle or two
had anything shiny been in the box.

You were Puss-In-Boots: skirts hiked up,
ready to swash buckles, to outsmart ogres —
a grin, a glint of blue eyes for steel,
one sturdy lace-up shoe toeing the bowsprit.

Cynicism took the starch out of me.
I was Rapunzel drooping in a kimono,
thinking how not to let down my hair and draw up
any more hangers-on. The joint was full already.

You went uptown. I went downhill,
and woke up with a jerk.
In the end we outsmarted an ogre or two,
lost our shirts (both stuffed and hair),

made our comebacks out of uniform.
Fifty years later, we grin at the camera —
swashing our buckles, laughing at dissonance.
No Cinderellas, just wiseacre heroines —

short on the spangles, but shining like stars.

FAT TIME

Under purest ultramarine the raised
goblets of trees overrun with gold.
We should be reeling drunk and portly as groundhogs
through these windfalls of russet, citron, bronze,
chartreuse.

Everywhere color pools like butter, like oil of ripe nuts
like piles of oranges under a striped tent.

Oh, let us be greedy of eyeball,
pigs scuffling in this gorgeous swill!
Let us cud this day
and spend the winter ruminant.

Let us write fat poems, and be careless.
Let us go bumbling about in wonder, legs
coated with goldenrod and smelling of acorns.

Let us be unctuous with scarlet and marigold,
larder them here, behind our foreheads
to glow in the brain's lamps
in the time of need.

Each tree a sun!
Let us throw away caution,
emblazon our retinas
with the flare and flame of it

so that in the unleavened winter
this vermilion spill, this skyfall,
these oils of tangerine, smears of ochre and maroon
will heat a spare poem, dazzle the eye's window,
feed us like holy deer on the blank canvas of snow.

MYOPIA IN THE AFTERNOON

What landscape is this? My flesh curving
over your bones, pectoral swell
under my cheek, darkness of tangled fur,
and beyond that, the wet

angled branch of a tree, and beyond that,
something white, something pale blue
Call it tree and window,
sky and snow.

But what this is, so close at hand, I cannot say.
This landscape of pleasure, where we fit together
this way, that way, it seems is nothing
I know, knew, can know —

only the rise and fall of breath,
the slow shifting of light on flesh,
and what has been, and what will come to be,
and here between them,
this.

FIREWORKS

Cars park in front of our house, sit there till midnight.
It's July, and hot. Rap thud, and rocket whine, and
the spit of firecrackers. We look out our window to see
the flash, then umbrellas of stars open red or green or
blue, sift down slowly onto the dark hill. Soft as rain.

I remember lying on the grass with my friend Kurt, as
running children called to one another in the dark-
ness, and the moment fell open around us — whistle
and thump and blossoming, and the drift of ash petals
onto our faces. Yet later, sitting in the open car, night
in our hair, we could not hold it. Fondness would not
catch fire

and we gave it up. Back at school he wrote a few times,
but friendship was nothing to me then, tenderness
was nothing, I was pursuing sex, power, and did not
have time for damp powder. Only now do I think of
him sometimes, his sweetness which was like your
sweetness.

Here in our bed tonight let us set match to fuse,
flame, blossom, open, drift like petals, and in our
hearts let there be the shapes of all who have ever
been there: lovers and friends, wives and husbands
and animals and children, pouring molten as stars
into what we are together.

BLESS YOU, FATHER WALT

for lying stripped and singing
in the floes and fallows of your own body.
For granting us land-rights to your shaggy
unkempt tongue
where through long syllables of scarlet leaves
we ride shanks-mare, drunk on the public road again.

Oh, bless me, Father Walt!
Lend me your large boots to caper and hoot at dusk,
make me shameless and grandiose
tender and foolish and brave.
Bless this false coin I use, stained as tinker's ware —
turn it to tigers resting in the shadows of my mouth.

22

Old Plow Horses

Today the tractor stands idle beside the barn.
The farmer is plowing in the old way.

The other horses gather against the fence,
stamping their massive legs, intent.

How silent it is. Only the creak of harness
and the soft *chk chk* of the man
and a nicker or slap of tail from the watching horses.

The grass is sweet
and the smell of old horses sweet and cheerful
where they crowd against the rail, leaning together.

Even the ancient ones seem young today,
the tides of their broad backs lifted,
heavy necks arched, ears pricked.

Such gleaming of dark eyes in the jonquil sunlight!
Such grave happiness in curve of neck and buttock!
Such tendriling out of knowledge
as if in stems and leaves!

November by Cazenovia Creek

Clear sky, flying clouds. Elsewhere
a terrible storm — tornados
in the southeast, hail in the Dakotas;
in Buffalo, high winds. But here
along the creek,
in thin late-afternoon sun,
in Arleen's woods,

only the sound of the river,
wind held in the cupped
hands of trees.
Molasses sunlight, a tang
of darkness. The afternoon
distilling. Over the creek,
one last dragonfly.

Leaf by leaf, stem by stem, wing
by wing, light releases
the thing it holds. Releases
the cups of my lifted hands —
spotted, knot-boned, odd
as an old branch. Thumb joints
like dragonflies.

A few late berries, a few asters,
and this bush with the light
behind it: nests of whitish fluff,
fibrous, coherent —
within each, a single dark seed.

SUDDEN OAK DEATH SYNDROME

Down the long body of California,
ramalina drapes the dead shoulders of oaks
with her bent hair.

Lace lichen. It's the color of sadness,
of rain that goes on for a long time,
of things fading into the distance.

Behind its veil ooze black
cankers of *phytophthora ramorum*.

We are in plague time now,
these dead too many to bury, shrouded
in lace the color of smog, fallen

like kindling over the stucco-colored hills,
behind dry lakebeds
where are tattooed the lost shapes of reeds.

Here I name them, the old friends:
live oak, scrub oak, white oak, black oak,
coffeeberry, huckleberry, buckeye, bay laurel,
rhododendron, manzanita, madrone, sequoia.

In the fires, even their roots will burn.

We leave our children a place with no eyelids.
They will die thirsty,
telling stories of our green shade.

THE OWL

The owl
on wide eyes of wings
carries out from shadow
the lank beast
of our secret
in her moon-
curved beak

beats behind us
as we run panting
takes us
our small bones
takes the nape
delicately
in her black hands

always
the owl comes sailing
out of the place we cannot look at
on easy wings
on currents of ice.

SPEAKING OF THE MUSE

My muse comes up behind me and says Honey
(she calls me honey)
you don't have a lot of time here —
lose the pale Flemish bride
with the sidelong glances.

She says Look! Here I am!
Dappled with oceans
furred with green and gold —
Honey, give me your full attention here!

O she turns
and light runs from her mountains
like sun off bleached bone
her mangrove hair winds in a sea of stars
on the round veldt of her belly elephants graze
and at her throat lie leopards,
waiting for me to come and drink.

She says You bring all those monkey voices
down here and leave them to the leopards.

She says You work your feet down deep in my mud
suck up that ripe swamp smell of life and death
and when the leopards come for you —
speak that, honey. Speak that.

II. The Hungry Ghost

BIRTH OF THE HUNGRY GHOST

Starveling flies in circles.
Gut flap, beak gape,
heart a hole,
bones of air.

Belly pumps once.
Egg falls down.
Starveling doesn't look back.
No food here.

Hungry child,
child of woe,
before, behind, above, below
no comfort anywhere.

Unweeping child.
Who would weeping call?
Nothing to catch and hold.
No food here.

Reaching, flailing,
icy arms at last
find herself, wind herself
tight, small, spare.

Closed egg again.
Hunger held within.
Heart a hole, bones of air:
empty as despair.

The Witch Rapunzel

Each year she armors herself more thickly
gives less
and less away.

From the tower of her body she sees only enemies.
Her eyes become gun turrets, her mouth
a murder-hole.

Though the strands
of her rosecolored hair
might be ladders

though she might slide
on their listening
out into the garden —

each year she thickens.
Each year she buries deeper
under scorched

earth
the bilecolored tears

for no one has saved her!
And it is not her fault!
She has been good, been good, been good, been good!

DEATH OF THE HUNGRY GHOST

Her skin hangs in strips
like dirty bandages.
Bruises pool and spread
over her balsa bones.
She smells of piss.

They come because they must.
From her metal nest
milky eyes turn
this way and that —
oh, a step! a kind word!

When their skins fall away
in strips like this
you will see the scars
on their throats
where she came for comfort.

GRIMM GHOST

Behind the drawn shade
your shadow blocks the moon.

Stands beside the cage.
Feels a finger for fatness.

Bends over the bed.
Chains of tear slime.

Oh sad jury-rigged monster
I shock-jolt you into breath,

undo the stitches of your bandages,
release you now.

Whatever raw thing shows itself
I declare you
harmless.

GRAVE OF THE HUNGRY GHOST

Over the ditched fen
one gray heron drifts
neck a catapult, beak a spear.

Among drowned sedge
two gray geese
mumble pale throats of grass.

In standing water
by broken trees
gravestones turn this way and that.

Under gravestones
float the gravid
like knuckled grasses knocking.

Ah   ah   ah
Remember
Me.

CODA

In the end
I have become the fairy godmother
the engine of all events
the wind.

Big-bellied with shadows
honeyed to the brow's
brim with water and words

I name the river
the leaf
the moon
the mother.

WHY HUNGRY GHOSTS MUST KEEP FLYING

Because they cannot rest

cannot dance strong fishbodies
through long brown kelp
or seep like sun through the tufted fingers of
redwoods

cannot breathe through their feet
or sprawl in hot sweet grass sated as seeds

cannot flicker out and in through their fingertips
making cloud-to-cloud lightning along the edges
of the world.

And in this place where throats are bells
clamoring the great sounding universe back to itself

they fly with throats clutched close
they drag empty dirigible bellies
their ears are filled with their own keening.

III. Sleeping Beauty

SLEEPING BEAUTY

All the godmothers have brought gifts
to the butterfly child.

Ghost flies in the window
crying   *Lack!   Lack!*

See the radiant child!
See how she is loved!

Ghost flies like a wasp
dry pain in her belly.
Her pinprick sows the radiant child with death.

O, the butterfly girl is dead between the ears.
Her breath ticks like a clock.
They make of her what they will.

But one day she will waken
with darkness and with light
with dancing and the cutting of knives.

She will slide from sleeping like a snake.

THE FINNMAN

She was dancing under the moon
in her small white bones

when the black finnman
rose up robed in water

and took her. In his house
no dancing no tide no moon.

There she suckled his babies
oh but not her own.

WHAT SHE LOST

Drowning
she did not look back
at the child abandoned on the shore.

Dull and shellshocked
as a lump of coal
she could not hear the child weeping.

She could not even hear
her own heart
as it came swimming out to free her.

IN THE COUNTRY OF THE DEAD

What can be said
on this side of the door?
Here where the trees have closed
their wings and the sea

has withdrawn behind its blue
tides and bed of wrack —
what voices could reach
me here? or what could I sing

of these walls and chairs
and clothes to be washed and meals
to be made
and how to keep

the ocean out
with its falling and rising
its bitter salt
the way it becomes

everything
sooner or later —
children's voices and
birds —

how
so heavy with
furniture
how can I keep
breathing

THE BUTTERFLY GIRL IS DEAD BETWEEN THE EARS

Not giving Kali her due.

Putting doll clothes on the old reptile head,
the flickering tongue and brain-stem eyes.

Housing anchorpeople behind the forehead.

Never
letting the hot rank breath of Kali
roar out the tongue's door

to blacken these pacified hills,
to make the sea boil and the prettylittlesails
candle and go out.

LOCAL HABITATION

From what rivers
do these pale
shapes crawl up
through drowned
branches, find
their blind
way to my throat
at last?

I cannot speak
for all of you!
I am not large
enough, steady
enough, cannot
even contain

the raw current
of my own grief
running like pitch
into the red gulf
of my mouth.

My Hump Speaks

I am the hunched rock
where no grace sits.
I am every twisted thing.

Splay foot, hay foot,
dog hit by stones.

Your throat hangs
from my hiding
like a suit on a hook.
Words dribble out
into the shadowed ground.

Within the umbrella
of twisted ribs,
caved, I wait.

Let me out.

I will lurch and uncoil.
I will fill you with noise.
I will open the blood-red
lily of your throat
and I will shout
No No No No No No No

JILL AND THE BEANSTALK

Jill is up the beanstalk all alone.
Only the chime of beans
in the dry pod.

She is hiding from the Ogre
behind the glitter
of His eyes.

She might be His very shadow,
exhaling His very breath
of rot and gnaw

and she is so small now,
wrapped in His black hide,
that she will never never be fou...

no no He has smelled her
He is upon her

but she takes up what she has found
and runs!
She is bringing it back, brave girl!

And with her own bright hatchet
she chops chops chops
through the roaring and the sky

shuddering
she chops chops chops

she keeps on chopping

THE ENDING

But it was I who set the planets in his hair!
It was I who rose from oceans of my own —
fish-goddess, shining woman!

I who offered him water, salt, and the moon's
changes. Instead he hangs, dry as a skate-fish,
far from the sea, his colors fading.

Yet under the crust, fire and water are one.
Sometimes behind his eyes I see something moving.
Sometimes on his breath I smell the salt of my skin.

Sometimes on my own tongue I taste his desert.

Song for a Dead Man

Plant you a wife, content to get
water or light, as you see fit.

Plant you a wife, content to grow
as you may prune her, high or low.

Plant you a wife. What you exhale
breath is to her! But if you fail —

what if she grapples earth to sky,
roots an ankle through each eye?

Kill her! Eat her! lest you wake
knowing what humus you will make

lest you hear her in the night
singing of rain and morning light

singing of earth and turning sun —
never of you. Or any one.

INANNA RETURNS

She comes out thin as root,
two black cubs shambling after.

She comes through the bright meadows
through bee song

to the place where he sits
on her throne, smeared
with honey and fat crumbs,
smelling of sex.

And she says:
Now you go.

WHAT THE RIVER SAYS

Who cannot go straight must go crooked.

Who cannot stand must go bent.

Who cannot sing must speak in a whisper.

Who goes alone will hear voices.

Who cannot let go must carry.

Who bears and is broken breaks open.

IV. In My Grandmother's Garden

EASTER MORNING

There they are where they fell, pricked
by the camera's spindle: side by side
in their starched dresses, patent leather shoes,
in sunlight, in somebody's garden.

The baby points eagerly toward the hidden egg —
bright-eyed, tufted as sparrow chick
hopping toward easter worm.
The elder turns inward on the pivot of a foot,

is familiar with egg-lure, has already practiced
the performance she will shortly give.
Still, some honesty of bone remains:
see the grip she takes of that small shoulder?

Stay back a while, the knuckles say.
The egg's a trap. Has closed on me. Stay free.

In My Grandmother's Garden

Under the lemon leaves I went to ground.
There headless fuchsias danced *en pointe*,
mad hibiscus spoke to me in tongues.
At evening, unharried to bath or table,
I snail-tracked in to bed a glamour
of rotting leaves and fell to darkness, unafraid.

No motherly earwig came whispering
and sucking at the brain, no Jerusalem
cricket scrabbled beside the bed,
weeping and wringing her claws,
though they crawled at night
from the garage's pale underbelly.

The summers floated like motes at midday,
but always they ended. I hid
in the jacaranda, or deep among orange thorns —
once, under the terrible garage.
Each year I was taken. I wonder
how I might have rooted, had I stayed.

MEMORY OF BESSIE FRAMED IN A MIRROR

It's a summer afternoon. Bessie stands
before a wood-framed mirror,
raising her arms to brush her hair.

Her ocean eyes smile, wrinkles deepen
beneath the still-clear arch of her brow.
She opens a golden tube and paints her lips.
(*Crimson. A word like soft velvet.*)

The child stands on a kitchen chair,
holding the mirror. "Salt and pepper,"
Bessie says, pinning up her hair.
(*Not a kitchen word! It's moonlight
springs from her temples.*)

Her bedroom smells of "Toujours Moi."
She raises the lid of an old trunk
and there, warm against white tissue

a long rope of hair, thick as her wrist,
glowing in the deepening light.
"Chestnut," she says,
(*a new word, whose syllables taste delicious —
like fire, like bread*)

"Chestnut. Like yours."
And the child at once becomes
beautiful as a rose.

The Inventor of the LuVailean Sonnet

She was no Millay, my Great-Aunt Lucy, but she
named herself Lyra LuVaile, Poet Laureate of Long
Beach, California, and wrote a book in which she
speaks familiarly of Stars, the Cosmos, the Music
of the Spheres ... subjects I might write about,
myself, though not perhaps so familiarly.

"The blood of Irish bards runs in our veins!" she
cried, upon hearing my baby self rhyme hop and stop.
(At which my grandmother whispered in my ear:
"Nonsense. We were *Orangemen*, my dear.")

Bony, ax-faced, that long Scotch-Irish nose — her
looks from her father, Jeremiah, the old man in the
daguerreotype with the rifle and Bible, the waist
length beard and the belt he used to whip them with.
All the girls looked like that — collarbones uneasy
under the frilly high-necked cambric, layers of ruffles
starched to fill out shirtwaist bodices — all except my
grandmother, small and dark and buxom. ("*I*," she
said, "*did not need ruffles.*")

But Lucy married at last, and moved out west with
her Calvinist husband, crippled in the First War, to
Long Beach, California — city of spiritualists and
faith healers, health regimens and Sears Roebuck
bungalows, where everything that had come a bit
loose across the vast prairies rolled until it hit the
water's edge — the LuVailean sonnet, for example,
which Lucy at once invented.

There she published her magazine, *Aeolian Harp*,
where poets who wrote of Veils and Starry Orbs
and Lyres might (for a fee) send their efforts to be
critiqued by the Laureate Herself, and if accepted
— which they were, after a few more go-rounds and
quite a few more fees — published, to the admiration
of their friends.

Well, she was no Millay, my Great-Aunt Lucy, but a
woman of parts, commercially speaking. And if she
said nothing about her actual life, the four neglected
children and the dark mean house, the smell of toilet
and unwashed clothes — if she escaped to her druids
and nymphs of fairy grace, her cerulean heavens and
sapphire seas, who can blame her?

(Except — what of the husband in his wheelchair
with his whipping cane? What of the monthly
envelopes full of cash, to pay her for the care of her
lost sister's secret child — money that kept a roof
over their heads, while day and night the boy was
beaten and beaten to drive out his mother's sin —
and herself not stopping it, not speaking a word of
love? Lucy, what of that?)

Our Father's Deafness

Sometimes our father sang to himself, about dusk on
the prairie and the slow murmur of cattle, about
rolling unshaven off a long-snaking train of flatbeds
with nothing but a tin can and a whistle.

There were two of us, and the poor mad bird
rocketing around the tall glass walls of the house
on a wheel of words. Behind his back she snaked her
neck and struck.

Then he was deaf. We thought him happy enough.
He had his work; we thought his deafness bought him
peace. But our father took to dying as sea grass takes
to salt.

Sometimes still I see his shadow, where darkness
shoulders up against the glass. He weighs the music
in each hand, turns the volume as high as it will go.

Then as the house rides out into the night on seas
and breakers of Beethoven, our father sits there hard
against the speakers, head cocked, eyes closed.
Listening.

LISTENING

Is the mother happy?
Will the mother come with her fists?
Will the mother come, sticky with tears?
Bad child! selfish child!
Child who does not love enough,
who does not make it all right, all right, all right.

Is the father happy?
Will the father stand in the doorway
calling don't, don't
as the mother hits, the mother screams?
In the night will the father cry out
with his bad dreams?
In the morning will they find him sobbing
I don't know what to do, I don't know what to do?

Is the little one happy?
Is the little one safe?
Will the little one wait, hunger,
hug her belly where it hurts?
Can she be comforted?
Or will she run out to her friends, brown and tough —
Leave me alone. I can take care of myself.

Even now my belly listens.
Even now my jaw smiles.
Even now my mouth answers:
Yes. Yes. Yes. Yes. Yes. Yes. Yes.

TRANSLATIONS

What word does it make, that calligraphy
of half-turned head and spine?
You stand in such privacy of bone
there in the doorway, looking back at me:

Sister. Your body speaks to me,
our Yoknapatawpha.
I too drift in its tides, sea-warm
as blood and thick with worlds.

Ah, we were cried forth in a black night
as lightning speaks from something broken
to name its territory, and yet
no word can tell me what I want to know,

not even this one:
heron-legged in the sun,
looking back at me,
between one thing and another.

V. Persephone Tells All

Rumpelstiltskin

You goatling, you manikin, you hobgoblin, you!
Remember how I sat closed in that gray tower,
heaped round with heavy heads of wheat
until my pale hands smelled of the sun?

Remember how the dead air filled
with golden dust, fragments of dark earth,
with pollen the color of honey?
Remember the nights? How the moth petals

flamed and shriveled, how the rushlights
stank of flesh from last night's banquet,
and how you sweated,
spinning all my harvest into coin?

And remember how you vanished
just as dawn fell in the window,
leaving me asleep amid a ruin of grain
my hair still meshed with the harsh silt of gold?

Oh, dance, tripartite meddler! Caper your wee feet!
But now I know your name,
and I will call you by it —
Infant! Husband! *Rumpelstiltskin!*

Ah. The coin uncoins, the walls dissolve
and I step through the gray stones
as simply as *this.*

CRONE STORY

Two men sat on a river bank
under a sage tree, fishing and talking
when up to them came an old crone walking
over the water, light as a leaf.

But when they threw out arms to ward her,
crying fear and their master's name
up she flew above their heads
on minnow wings and blithely said,

"Surely your mothers taught you ill
if they did not tell their sons
how out of fishy water comes
soon or late the old girl walking —

how goodwives turn their coats and swim
among the toothy roots again
how they come walking in the end
over water to frighten men."

"Hag!" they cried and took up fire
and burned the tree and the old one in it.
Away they ran from the river bank,
and the river's voice like a crow.

But as from blackened wood in spring
green leaves of sage rise up again,
along on the goodwife's twiggy canes
comes the young girl walking to welcome them.

Persephone Tells All

Persephone carried off (faintly protesting)
by Big Beard the Muscleman,
her weeping mother searched
round and round
but did not go down
town. Which is where she was.

But Big Beard down there
in the lamplight
in the altogether
was altogether
so large, so loud,
and the latesummer heat so oppressive,
Persephone got tired of it (though liking the Harley
okay)
so she took a hike.

"I wanted a big man," she says,
"someone who took up the space —
someone who knew what he thought,
so I didn't have to,
you know,

think. It was cool I guess
with the jewels and zombies and all that —
but after a while the oxygen
was running short
with all that hot air
and after a while he got heavy —
like *I* could ever be on top —

and after a while you notice
how they are always
going on and on and on
about *themselves*,
know what I mean?"

THE REAL STORY

It is reported by the castle press agent
that the stepsisters have cut off their toes
to fit inside a glass slipper
leaving a trail of blood behind their horses
by which they have been discovered.

Oh, false princesses!
They will never live in the palace with the prince
(such a fine boyo, too
in his wind-up codpiece and padded doublet).

But wait! Back on the road
the sisters look down at the drops
falling between their hooves
which are blossoming into dragons

and the cross-
dressing god-
mother slips out of town

while the paper dolls
in their pink foil balldresses and origami doublets
are left hanging by tabs
from an otherwise thin story line

and from every corner of the Real
World the dragons come

dancing and hollering
on their big
imperfect
scaly
thick-toed
feet.

THE MERMAID SINGS

The coiled muscle ripples. Stars and moons
mirror and regard themselves in her bright scales.

She calls no one to her by her singing.
She saves no one, destroys no one.

It's like this: from her mother's body
she slipped into the current, her mouth opened,
she sang.

There's no reason for her tail, either.

VI. Monkeypod Suite

Hilo Farmers' Market

Under the awning, packed voices —
Hawaiian, Pidgin, Japanese, Portuguese,
Thai, Korean, Chinese....
Saturday morning, everyone
comes to market:
aunties and uncles, tourists
in their hats, babies in strollers,
Japanese grandmothers
shopping for the family,
and me, *haole* grandmother,
drifting, eating

words. On the tables, piles
of words – *lilikoi* and *lychee*,
red *alaea* salt from which
the first man was made, *taro*
for baking and for *poi*, *ti* leaves
for wrapping *lau lau* —

and the canoe plants: dried *ava ava*
and bananas – *lele* – tied in bunches,
giant *ulu* fruit and sweet potato, *'uala*,
sacred to pig-nosed Kamapua'a —

nosegays of orchids and *kinnamoni*,
kuavas and *poha* berries, bright red *rambutan* —
and young green coconuts — *niu* —
with straws stuck in so you can drink the water —
and *papayas*, piles and piles of *papayas*,
a bag for a dollar —

tubs of coconut *haupia* pudding,
of pink and green *mochi* and *tapioca*
and jars of *mamane* honey
and *ohelo* berry jam,

then *bento* boxes, *kim chee*, *pad thai*
and rows and rows of seaweed-banded
musubi — spam *musubi*, shrimp *musubi* —

and purple *poi* and dried *ahi*,
salt *tako poke* and *ahi poke*,
and sometimes, on ice, fresh *ono*
which is also the word for delicious —

and *kope* by the cup, and *kope* beans —
local *kope*, better than Kona,
kope from Ka'u and Hamakua —

and I drifting, eating
mouth-shapes — light and dark, sweet
and salty, rivers of *l* and *e* and *i*
throat-caught with glottals, staccatoed
with *k* and *p* —

Hilo throat-song,
tongue-binding all this color,
odor, sound —
and I in the middle
drifting, blissful,
dumb.

My Fat Zumba Teacher

She is rich in flesh, ripe and bursting
as a guava, a lychee, a kona
avocado. She is full of sex
and pleasure, she rolls her hips
and shimmies, she shakes
her belly and the place
where the jelly roll rolls.

Behind her stand
the generations of dancers,
halaus of wisewomen —
heavy-thighed, strong-throated,
weighty on the platform,
their hands talking story,
their bodies full
of all they remember.

On the black sand
at Richardson's Beach
they play in the surf,
swim like dolphins. Like *honu*.
They float. I float.
We sit under coconut trees
and laugh
and shout to one another
and eat.

MONKEYPOD SUITE

i
A full moon rests in the morning sky over Mauna Kea.
Here below, the monkeypod tree is netted with silver.

The sun appears as a campfire over the ocean.
To the south, in Puna, clouds gather.

Behind the dark lattice of the monkeypod tree,
pale orange sherbet, lemon ice.

ii
At sunrise, floating above the clouds:
Mauna Kea, pink with snow.

To the west crouches the other mountain:
Mauna Loa. Still alive. Waiting.

iii
Hilo town —
Japanese town,
jungle town,
sugar town,

tumbledown
from rain and damp-rot,
tsunamis and shaking —

origami moth
hung between burning
and drowning.

iv
Windward means *wet*.
Means storms, orchids, *monstera deliciosa*,
means unpacific waves that wipe out harbors:
no foothold here, small fry.

v
Always the earth shudders, giving birth.
Hilo sways like a red bird on a stem of bamboo.

vi
Everyone knows it will come some day,
like the ones in '46, in '60,
that sucked the water out of Hilo harbor
and then came in again —
huge, silent, terrible as God.

vii
When the wind shifts,
vog eats at the lungs —
sulfur from Kilauea.

But it is Mauna Loa we fear:
some day, down all the bright waterfalls:
fire.

viii
This is why the monkeypod
shivers continually,
why Hilo rests so lightly —
a moth, an origami rainbow —
over its rain-sweet curve of bay.

El Niño Winter, Hilo

Wet black firerock, porous and sharp
green orchids and green trunks and thick red ginger
and white buds of coral, tiny as eyelashes

and riptide catching
the ankles, and cold green foam
and early dark, and rain —

gray rain and early dark
and the mob stink of lynchrope vines
and the jungle closing in

against the small ribs of the chest and

you dream of barren places, high places,
wide light, silica
you dream of breathing

but rain batters the tin skull of the house
and gobbles up the dawn

and neon orchids and long-penised anthuriums
and monstera and poison-sapped vines grow

incessant fingers into the walls of the house
and will eat it
and will eat you.

ON HILO BAY

In the tidepools
of Coconut Island
redgold koi are swimming —
floating leaves
from the *kamani haole* trees.

At nightfall
boys cast out from black rocks
draw up
dark shapes struggling,
thick as their arms.

TRADEWIND RAIN

Noise takes the house
the way a wave will take a thing
and leave it mindless.

And then it blows out
east through the harbor
and through the crack of dawn

where lavender and rosegold
rise from tomorrow

and the birds say something
to one another
and you go back to sleep.

WALKING AKOLEA ROAD

Two cardinals in blue ginger.
Three mynahs on a rock wall.

Red cocks crow, compare tailfeathers,
herd their households along the street.

Back then, the kids called it the Burma Road.
Sugar cane hid the sky, sweetest when tasseling.

Now Mauna Kea shines above pastureland,
and down in the blue harbor, a ship has come in.

In a plowed field of bright rust-colored earth
men in woven hats are planting ginger stalks.

Flocks of little yellow birds consult in the wild cane.
In the sun, the sweet smell of molasses grass.

Three horses, two bays and a buckskin
amble down to the fence to be sweet-talked.

An old woman is walking her goat on a leash.
A cockatoo and a blue parrot ride on her shoulders.

VII. Packing for the Journey

PACKING FOR THE JOURNEY

One morning she comes up knowing
that she can only take the big snake
and the cactus with her in the car —

that she has to leave all the animals behind
because the car is packed full of everyone's things
so there is only room for the sleeping coils

of the great shadowed snake in her basket
and the saguaro with its two arms sticking upright
which is suspended from a hanger
in the back window.

And she knows why the snake is there.
But she wonders about the cactus.

FOOL ON THE BANK OF THE RIVER STYX

Must I stand by this river weeping
for the lost otter of the body?

Think of the ragged moon,
suffusing all the world with milky radiance!

And if it has taken me so long to get here —
so long that now I must caper vegetable flesh,

flapping these Caliban arms
and the dry breasts of the crone —

still the Fool sets out along the river's edge,
shaking her rattle and walking on her hands,

dancing what she does not know to dance.

THE WHITE QUEEN

      Comes the White Queen worrying
and hurrying to keep up and losing
her hairpins. Mind pieces slip
out of their sockets.

      Because it is all held together
with hairpins —
the old kind,
meant to be invisible

      and they *were* invisible.
I didn't know they were there holding
my mind together
until I started to lose it.

      Someone whose name I should remember
talks of the sweet dishevelment of love,
but this dishevelment
is not sweet.

      Or perhaps I am wrong,
perhaps I should

      no, *could*, because one should speak
only in possibilities not rules
but where was I

      I *could* perhaps experience
this dishevelment as sweet —
this mental coming apart

or opening up, which is a more
appealing concept. The mind dropping hairpins,
not in the process of falling

off in chunks
but of opening up.
Light through the cracks.

So this dropping
off of things — of memory,
cleverness, concentration —
perhaps is not matter for grief but sign
of expansion.

If poetry cannot be made,
perhaps it will come in
as a gift. Joy
creating everything,
even this.

Even the White Queen,
silly and confused and showering
silver hairpins so beautiful and full of light.

MY LIFE IN MATHEMATICS

My third grade teacher fissioned us into teams.
Flashed cards. Shouted. Five seconds to answer:
7 times 8! *Ruth! Five! Four! Three! Two! One!*

My team always lost. A brain can be a cloud chamber
full of random events. And shame is easy to memorize.

Later, my mother drilled me with flash cards in a
hotel room in Sweden in a rage because I still could
not memorize the multiplication tables

yet I remember clearly how it smelled there beside
the vast gray lake, and how in the empty dining room
light circled as though in clouds

and I remember the smell of my mother's anger, and
what she wanted from me.

In college I passed statistics only through the patient
tutoring of the professor, a young man, worried and
awkward and kind.

Because I was pretty. I do remember that.

In the end I worked out a way to cheat on the
multiplication tables, and I have used it all my life.
The numbers are shaped like the bones in my body,

though I cannot tell you how. Perhaps I knew, once,
but memory slips away now like a fish you can see
moving under water, sliding past the hook.

Yet I believe what we know in the bones will stay with
us — like the face of a young man kind and awkward
in his stiff professor's suit, and not much older than I

and how I must have looked, sitting across from him
in my new spring dress — oh, pretty, and quick,
and brief as a flower.

A May Afternoon at the Poets' Group

It begins with listening to a tape in the car and just
as it gets to the sexy part
The tape slows into that mush-mouth dying-tape
sound: *ryaaoawraaaeeeo.*
In the garden, a sestina (sextina, sextain) is read,
which (by any other name) has sex in it.
And before our eyes an insect is laying her eggs in
delicate shining ooze,
Which though not a sestina is certainly a kind of
poetry,
To which even those locked in the Memory Unit still
have the key, though maybe not for long.

Yet fearlessly a bright yellow dandelion flaunts in the
field of green, and before long,
In someone's imaginary town the village clerk is
taking pictures of Sharon Brown's sexy parts,
While in our own neighborhood a laboring pianist
has got the metronome in her teeth now and is laying
eggs of tedium which might, in another galaxy, be
poetry,
And the bus to Trivandrum downshifts in memory
with a sound of straining gears: *ryaaoawraaaeeeo*
(And there was a child throwing up on the bus,
though not making such a delicate shining ooze
As this tiny-legged insect laying her eggs on the
magenta phlox, which has so much sex in it.)

Somewhere else is a landscape of poison-sapped vines,
which has both death and sex in it,

But here none of us are dead – though one could be
struck dumb by a day like this! But not for long.
Because somewhere between metronomic laboring
and a kind of meaningless ooze
Is the part never revealed by the Hubble, which is to
say: the poetry part.
(Arnaud Daniel, for example, who made sestinas in
the *lang d'oc* – which if slowed by the passage of
centuries might sound like *ryaaoawraaaeeeo* –
Only with an *accent grave* on the second syllable,
which makes it Poetry.)

And that is what we are having, on this perfectly
natural day: poetry.
Which inevitably, like everything else, has loss and
time and death and sex in it.
Where even someone screaming in the Memory Unit
begins to run down into a slur of: *ryaaoawraaaeeeo*.
And here in our garden the metronome and the
neighbor's sunflowers and Blackie the dog will soon
say *So long*
(Like the poetry of making silly rabbit faces, which so
entranced the careening busload of Muslim children
that at the end of the journey they would not depart).
And slowly, naturally, the hours float away through
galaxies of shining ooze

And begin to erase: *ryaaoawraaaeeeo*. For this is
poetry,
Which begins in ooze shining and blooming and
with sex in it,
And no matter how much we long to stay, too soon we
part.

94

DRIFTWOOD

Eyes touch first: shape of a bird,
a hole, a small darkness.

Scent of dust. Taste of wood.
To the fingers, carved rivulets.

Almost weightless — all water gone.
But held against the ear, a sound of water.

Bird shape: tailed, curved, close-winged.
Or a dolphin face: lower lip, eye.

Or, turned over, a cupped hand,
fits to my own hand, shape to shape.

From seed, root, sapling, tree,
from spreading, breaking, falling, bearing,
from rock, water, heat, hands

we are made new. Worn away.
This space within.

SOMEONE WILL REMEMBER US

(Fragments by Sappho from *If Not, Winter*, translated by
Anne Carson)

Someone will remember us
I say
even in another time.

Red bird with lapis eyes
at Eftalou, on Lesvos, looking
into sunrise and the Turkish coast

remember how our narrow arches
left half-hoofprints in the sand
how when we rose from the foam

in moonlight, we were made of shells,
ivory and pearl, eyes black ebony,
gold ankle bones.

ON SANTA MONICA BEACH

A Riddle in Two Voices

That they were wet.
> *That they were shining.*

That they moved.
> *Like fish under water.*

That they were the color of apricots.
> *Of tigers in the sunset.*

That they spoke so fluently.
> *As fingers speak to fingers.*

That they were slender.
> *Empty as the new moon.*

That they had released themselves.
> *That they had fallen.*

That they were reduced to
> *Yes. This.*

Answer: They are shells.

Humus

Let the space
between tree and "tree"
be humus.

Let the space between us
fill with roots
that are (not) mine.

Let form come from this exact
place, be knit
to this tree's branching
as close as bark.

Because nothing is another thing
or a puppy of our thoughts
but only this
happening here between us:

let me grow a word for this.

VIII. Sometimes in Dreams

Journeying West

Journeying west to a new country,
women mark the trails
with the things they leave behind.
Fans, little papers of rice powder,
fine-laced shoes, tucked
petticoats — almost at once they find
things they can do without.

Mired in the silt of rivers
they leave the familiar
anchors of mirrors and featherbeds,
the barrels of salt pork and windfall cider
they put up against winter.

Then muddled by distance
or the way the prairie
continually withdraws from them,
or because the stars here blossom in strange places,
they leave behind the failed
compasses of letters, of bibles

and somewhere in the desert
they abandon the shallow
graves, the broken
axles
of memory
and desire.

So in the end
women leave behind everything
but what is in their heads.
And then even
what is in their heads —

climbing the next
rock, the narrow trail,
smelling water and going to it —

in this way women cross the mountains,
and bring themselves down to the sea.

Travel Instructions for Elmwood Avenue

You leave the sepia light of the tea restaurant,
lapsang and peony, earth and green twig,
continuo of quiet human voices.

Outside is rain, fat frying, damp exhaust, sputum,
spit of tires on a wet street, brakes tuned
to the pulse of streetlights: green, amber, red, green.

You blunder, glasses fringed with rainbows,
until your own hands swim out before you —
greeny in the headlights, strange as ectoplasm.

Light laps from shattered planes of reflection,
emerges and re-emerges from sheeting brilliance.
Dimension becomes dimension, a turned fan.

Now darkness hums like a bowed string,
anchored somewhere you cannot see,
one end floating here in the spinning world

and what has always sung from around the corner
is no longer apart from you —
it is here, upon you — that blaze of tenderness!

FOR CIRCE

Circe, take care. I know that charm you make.
Such wit was mine as furnishes your feast.
You'd give a lilt to crow-call, clip their wings,
turn drowned strangers into beasts.

When they but sigh your name, and no more rise
to fling their private lark-song down the air,
but lie about you trussed, your face their sun —
ah, that's a swiny mirror, Circe. Take care.

Alone, you'll dream of alien chemistries
riding salt currents to mount your flickering tongue,
of kelp-rope bleeding, binding skin to skin,
of darkness rising, opening lung to lung.

Here's truth: unbound, Odysseus escapes,
the lark beats up and up on glittering wings.
All you may keep is chancy overheard:
will how you will, you will not make them sing.

Salt-self each self goes forth. Like dolphins in that sea
each knows what each can know. Our dying sets us
free.
The current turns, my child. Let go your mirrors
and drown.
It sings at root of ocean, though every lark be flown.

AT GHOST RANCH

I am a watermark in a rimmed valley,
a kite become cloud.

By day the bent bowl of blue
pours hot gold through my body.

By night the knelt darkness
pours milk of stars.

If I am a shape held together
by water and the memory of water —
when water quits me, who am I?

The sun calls it out of me —
leaping into that blue eye.

If I lie like a scent upon this place,
if the lake of blue percolates through me,
will I gather moisture, begin

to cohere? Will I collect
into myself? Or something
I do not know?

I Am Here To Tell You

you will be amazed
to find yourself smelling that swampy
muskrat spring again

to be wriggling your tail again
through water browngold with washed
sediment of mines —
oh do your work rightly
and come back here full of tales
(dropping off and growing legs)

sit yourself on something green
roll up a few thisnthats on your tongue
and watch the sky go by
rocking

a thigh to the music
of kingfishers
dragonflies
black stones slippery with algae
slow mud dissolving.

Dream of the Snow Leopard

At a stop light
in the front seat of the car beside me
a snow leopard sits
looking out the window.

He regards me for a moment —
relaxed, green-eyed,
detached as snow melt —
and vanishes as the light changes.

Milarepa went alone, it is said,
into the cave of demons.
Next morning, when they came for him,
the cave was empty

save for a snow leopard
to which,
being wise men,
they bowed.

MINE

small sunflower
goldtoes

little ocean
skyeyes

on my hip
riding

never lost.

SOMETIMES IN DREAMS YOU SEE WINGS

Sometimes you wake to a wing of rain
coming in slantwise under clouds
to muscled light
and the sound of crows.

Or sometimes late in life you turn
and see the landscape you have become
spreading out behind you
like a leaf unfolding, or a wing.

Sometimes in dreams you see
that the air is made of wings
that oceans are glittering scales
that shadows are wombs and graveyards honeycombs

that the earth is swaying and brushing up against you
that all of it is singing.

Acknowledgements

With gratitude to all who have read, listened, advised, and encouraged, especially:

Mary Brown, Irving Feldman, Carol Flynn, Ann Goldsmith, Nancy Hunt-Coffey, Frank X. Gaspar, Don Mitchell, Stanley Plumly, Judith Slater, Philip Terman

and the women of AROHO.

Grateful acknowledgment is made to the editors of the following magazines, anthologies and awards:

2010 Writers' Digest Poetry Awards: "The Witch Rapunzel."

Beyond Bones: "El Nino Winter," "Monkeypod Suite," "My Fat Zumba Teacher," "On Hilo Bay," "Tradewind Rain."

Chautauqua: "Myopia in the Afternoon," "Old Plow Horses," "Sometimes In Dreams You See Wings," "Why Hungry Ghosts Must Keep Flying."

Clackamas Literary Review: "Our Father's Deafness."

The Comstock Review: "Rumpelstiltskin."

Earth's Daughters: "Dream of the Snow Leopard," "Someone Will Remember Us."

Eclipse: "Bless You, Father Walt," "Translations."

Harpur Palate: "The Owl," "Sudden Oak Death Syndrome."

Naugatuck River Review: "In My Grandmother's Garden."

New Millennium Writings: "Fat Time," "Second Childhood," and "Speaking of the Muse."

Poetry, Memoir, Story: "On Santa Monica Beach."

Potomac Review: "Woman With Crows."

Sow's Ear Poetry Review: "Journeying West."

Thirteenth Moon: "Easter Morning."

"Fat Time" won the *New Millennium Writings* Poetry Award in 2007.

"The Owl" won the *Harpur Palate* Milton Kessler Award in 2010.

"A May Afternoon at the Poets' Group" won the Chautauqua Mary Jane Irion Prize in 2009.

Woman with Crows was a finalist for the AROHO Foundation *To the Lighthouse* Poetry Book Prize in 2010.

About the author

Ruth Thompson grew up in California and received a BA from Stanford and a PhD from Indiana University. She has been an English professor, librarian, college dean, and yoga teacher in Los Angeles. She now lives in Hilo, Hawai'i, where she teaches writing, meditation, and yoga.

Her poems have won the *New Millennium Writings* Poetry Award and the *Harpur Palate* Milton Kessler Memorial Prize, among others.

Woman with Crows is her second book of poetry, and was a finalist for the A Room of Her Own Foundation's *To The Lighthouse* Prize in 2010. Her chapbook, *Here Along Cazenovia Creek* (Saddle Road Press, 2011), was the basis for a collaborative performance of poetry and dance with Japanese dancer Shizuno Nasu.

Her website is at http://ruththompson.net